The Greenwich Guide to
Time and the
Millennium

Graham Dolan

Heinemann Library
Des Plaines, Illinois

GREENWICH
MERIDIAN
2 | 000

Some words are shown in bold, **like this.** You can find out what they mean by looking in the glossary.

1999 Reed Educational & Professional Publishing
Published by Heinemann Library,
an imprint of Reed Educational & Professional Publishing,
1350 East Touhy Avenue, Suite 240 West
Des Plaines, IL 60018

© National Maritime Museum 1999

Designed by Susan Clarke
Illustrations by Jeff Edwards
Printed in Hong Kong by Wing King Tong Co. Ltd.

03 02 01 00 99
10 9 8 7 6 5 4 3 2 1

Library of Congress Cataloging in Publication Data

Dolan, Graham. 1953–
    The Greenwich guide to time and the millennium / Graham Dolan.
        p.   cm.
    Includes bibliographical references and index.
    Summary: Examines different aspects of time and how we measure it, including seasons, sundials, clocks, local and Greenwich mean time, the prime meridian, time zones, atomic clocks, months, years, and more.
    ISBN 1-57572-802-8 (lib. bdg.)
    1. Time–Juvenile Literature. 2. Time measurements–Juvenile literature.   [1. Time. 2. Time measurements.]   I.   Title.
QB209.5.D65   1999
529–dc21   98-43198
                                                                CIP
                                                                AC

Acknowledgments

The Publishers would like to thank the following for permission to reproduce photographs: Bridgeman Art Library, pp. 41 (top), 44; Giraudon, p. 40; British Library, p. 15 (middle); Francisco Diego, p. 42; Robert Harding Picture Library/M. Bolster, p. 37; National Maritime Museum, pp. 4 (top), 10, 11 (bottom), 14 (all), 15 (top and bottom), 16 (both), 17 (both), 19, 20, 22 (both), 23 (bottom), 24, 26, 28 (both), 29 (all), 31 (both), 36, 45 (top right and bottom); Powerhouse Museum, Sydney, p. 23 (top); Science Museum/Science and Society Picture Library, p. 12 (both); G. Bernard, p. 34; NASA, p. 5; D. van Ravenswaay, p. 4 (bottom); F. Sauze, p. 11 (top); Sipa Press/I. Simon p. 45 (top left); Studio Carr Ltd, p. 37 (top); Syndics of Cambridge University Library and the Director of The Royal Observatories, p. 27; John Webb, p. 41 (bottom).

Cover: Chris Honeywell (center); National Maritime Museum (top left, top right); Science Photo Library/Detlev van Ravenswaay, (lower left); NASA/Science Photo Library, (bottom right).© National Maritime Museum (1999)

Every effort has been made to contact copyright holders of any material reproduced in this book. Any omissions will be rectified in subsequent printings if notice is given to the Publisher.

Contents

The Earth:
Our Timekeeper

Hundreds and thousands of years

A period of 100 years is called a **century,** and a period of 1,000 is called a **millennium.** Few people who are alive today will live long enough to celebrate their one hundredth birthday, but most people will still be alive in the year 2000. They will take part in celebrations welcoming in a new millennium.

The Millennium Dome at Greenwich in London, England, under construction in 1998.

The length of a year

Our year is based on the length of time it takes for the earth to go around, or **orbit**, the sun once. The farther a planet is from the sun, the longer it takes to complete one orbit. If the earth were as close to the sun as the planet Mercury, each earth year would be about one quarter as long. If, on the other hand, we were as far away as the farthest planet, Pluto, each earth year would be about 250 times as long. If that were the case, you wouldn't live to see your first birthday.

This is our solar system.

4

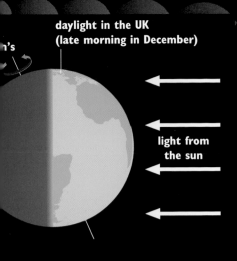

daylight in the UK
(late morning in December)

light from
the sun

ht in the UK
e early hours of the following morning)

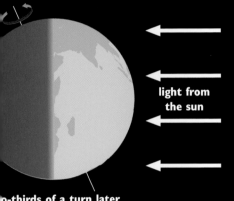

light from
the sun

o-thirds of a turn later

Half of the earth is always in darkness.

The earth spins around on its axis just more than 365 times in one orbit around the sun.

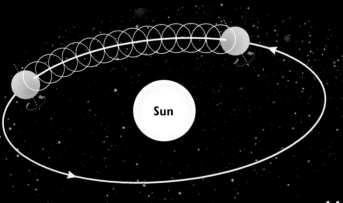

Sun

This is the earth photographed from space. The left side is facing away from the sun and is in darkness.

Day and night

At the same time as it orbits the sun, the earth is spinning on its **axis**. When the part of the earth we are on is facing towards the sun, we receive light and energy from the sun. We call it daytime. As the earth spins, we eventually end up facing away from the sun. When this happens, light and energy from the sun can no longer reach us. It goes dark and night begins.

The number of days in a year

The length of time that we call a day is just about the same as the time it takes for the earth to spin around once on its axis. Each day is divided into 24 hours. Each hour is divided into 60 minutes. And each minute is divided into 60 seconds. In the time it takes the earth to orbit the sun once, the earth spins on its axis just over 365 times. Because the length of a year is really about 365¼ days, some calendar years are given 365 days. Others, called **leap years,** are given 366 days. Leap years normally occur every four years. If the earth were spinning faster, the days would be shorter and there would be more days each year. If, though, the earth were spinning more slowly, the days would last longer. Each hour, minute, and second would be longer, and our clocks would have to tick more slowly.

Summer and Winter

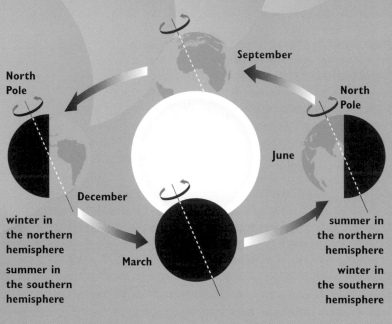

North Pole

September

North Pole

June

December

March

winter in
the northern
hemisphere

summer in
the southern
hemisphere

summer in
the northern
hemisphere

winter in
the southern
hemisphere

The earth leans as it makes its journey around the sun. As the earth moves around its **orbit**, the direction in which its **axis** points hardly changes. This means that when it is on one side of its orbit, the North Pole points towards the sun. When it is on the opposite side of its orbit, the North Pole points away from the sun and the South Pole points towards it.

Summer and winter are at different times of the year in the northern and southern hemispheres.

Hot and cold

When the North Pole points towards the sun, people in the United States, Canada, and other places in the more northern parts of the northern hemisphere, called the northern **temperate zone**, get warmer weather. When the North Pole points away from the sun, it gets colder weather. We call the period of warmer weather *summer*, and the period of colder weather *winter*.

The more hours of daylight there are each day, the greater the amount of energy received from the sun.

darkness

daylight

North Pole

Sun

daylight

darkness

North Pole

When the North Pole points away from the sun (December), people in the northern temperate zone get less hours of daylight than darkness each day.

When the North Pole points towards the sun (June), people in the northern tempera zone get more hours of dayligh than darkness each day.

6

Why, though, should it be hotter or colder just because the North Pole is pointing towards or away from the sun? In the northern temperate zone, when the North Pole points towards the sun, there are more hours of daylight each day. The sun rises higher in the sky. This means that the earth receives more energy each day and it is hotter.

In countries in the southern temperate zone, such as Uruguay and New Zealand, summer occurs when the South Pole is pointing towards the sun. When this happens, the North Pole will be pointing away from the sun. The countries in the northern temperate zone will be having winter.

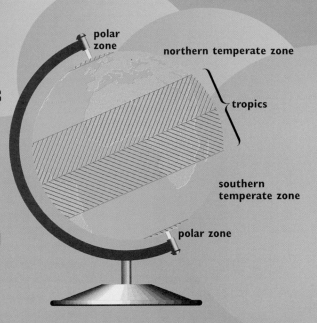

The solstices and the equinoxes

In the northern temperate zone, the summer solstice occurs around June 21. The sun reaches its highest **midday** point of the year. Six months later, on about December 21, the winter solstice occurs. The sun reaches its lowest midday point of the year. The amount of daylight increases each day between the date of the winter solstice and the date of the summer solstice. It then begins to decrease again. About halfway between the solstices—around March 21 and September 22—the equinoxes occur and everyone around the world gets equal amounts of daylight and darkness. In the southern temperate zone, the sun reaches its highest midday point in December and its lowest midday point in June.

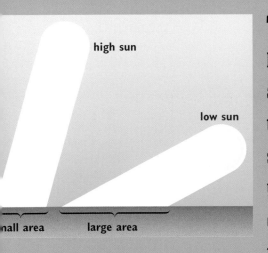

When the sun is higher in the sky, its energy is concentrated over a smaller area of the earth's surface. So, it will be warmer.

The Sun's Movement
Across the Sky

The sun appears to move from east to west

As the earth spins on its **axis**, the sun and the stars appear to move across the sky in a curve from east to west. At **midday** in the northern **temperate zone**, the sun is in the south and the shadows point towards the north. In the southern temperate zone, things are reversed. The midday sun is in the north and the shadows point towards the south.

In the **tropics**, it is very different. The midday sun is in the south during the period around December 21 but in the north during the period around June 21. On the **equator**, the midday sun is directly overhead at the time of the equinoxes in March and September.

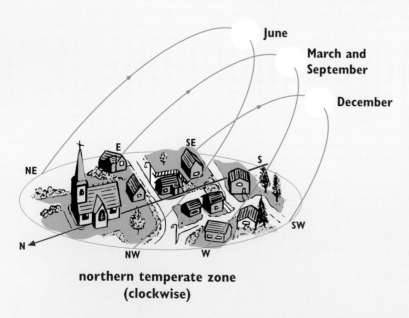

northern temperate zone
(clockwise)

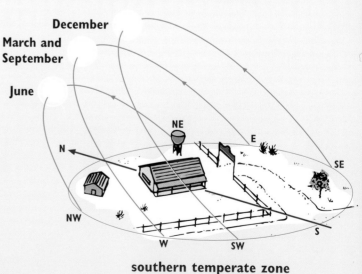

southern temperate zone
(counterclockwise)

These diagrams show the path of the sun across the sky.

Shadows

As the sun rises in the sky, the length of a shadow gets shorter and shorter. By midday, when the sun is at its highest point of the day, the shadows are at their shortest. Then they start to get longer again, increasing in length all the time until the sun sets. As the sun moves across the sky, the direction of the shadows changes, too. The shadows are always on the opposite side of the sun. In the morning when the sun is in the east, shadows point toward the west. In the evening when the sun is in the west, shadows point toward the east.

Meridian lines

No matter where you are, the shadows at midday always fall along a north–south line. One end of the shadow points toward the earth's North Pole, and the other end points toward its South Pole. North–south lines are known as **meridians** or meridian lines. They are very important when finding the time from observations of the sun or the stars.

The length and direction of a shadow depends on where the sun is in the sky.

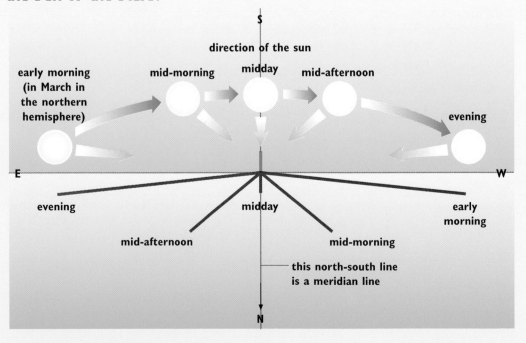

Sundials

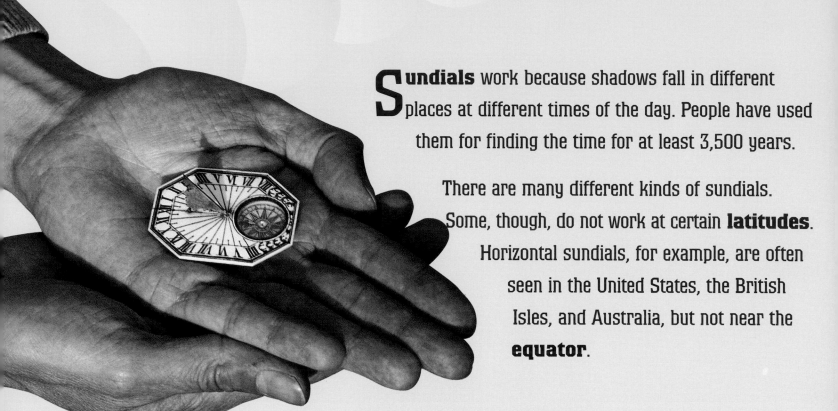

Sundials work because shadows fall in different places at different times of the day. People have used them for finding the time for at least 3,500 years.

There are many different kinds of sundials. Some, though, do not work at certain **latitudes**. Horizontal sundials, for example, are often seen in the United States, the British Isles, and Australia, but not near the **equator**.

Portable sundials like this were used from about the mid-sixteenth **century** until the first half of the nineteenth century, when accurate watches became more widely available. This French sundial is more than 300 years old.

Hours of unequal length

Many of the oldest surviving sundials were marked to divide the period of daylight into twelve hours. Until the fourteenth century, the day in many countries was divided this way. The length of each daylight hour and each nighttime hour varied with the seasons. Daytime hours were longer in the summer than in the winter.

Hours of equal length

The invention of the mechanical clock eventually led to our days being divided into hours of equal length. Hours recorded by most clocks consist of the same number of evenly spaced ticks. Therefore, they are always the same length.

In the past, vertical sundials were the most common type. They were attached to the outside walls of buildings at a height so they couldn't be easily touched. The spacing of the hour marks depends on both the sundial's latitude and the direction that the wall is facing.

As more and more clocks were built, more and more sundials were marked to show equal hours, too. Until the twentieth century, most people relied on a sundial to set their clocks and watches to the right time.

This horizontal sundial was made in 1582 for use in a garden in the northern hemisphere. The numbers are marked in a clockwise direction. If it had been made for use in the southern hemisphere, the tip of the gnomon would point towards the south and the numbers would be marked in a counterclockwise direction.

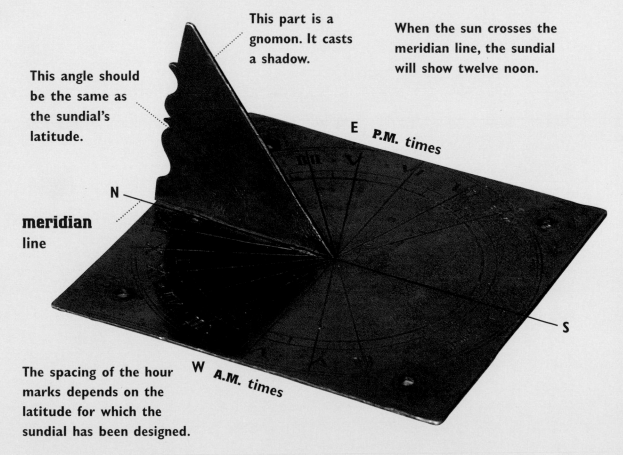

This part is a gnomon. It casts a shadow.

This angle should be the same as the sundial's latitude.

When the sun crosses the meridian line, the sundial will show twelve noon.

E P.M. times

N

meridian line

S

W A.M. times

The spacing of the hour marks depends on the latitude for which the sundial has been designed.

The First Clocks

One of the problems with a **sundial** was that it couldn't tell time at night or when the sun was not shining. Even in the sunniest places, sundials couldn't be used for long periods of time. The solution was building timekeepers—devices that allowed people to keep track of time when they were unable to find it directly from the sun or the stars.

Water clocks

One of the earliest timekeepers was a container full of water with a hole in the bottom. Water clocks were used in the monasteries of Europe for many hundreds of years. They were used to ensure that bells were rung at the right time to wake the monks and call them to prayer throughout the day.

Water clocks, like this model, were used in temples in Egypt about 3,400 years ago. Inside, there are different scales for different times of the year. This is because the length of each "Egyptian hour" varied with the seasons.

This modern model shows part of a giant water clock that was completed in China in 1092. The waterwheel turned with a series of stop-start movements or "ticks."

The first mechanical clocks

The first mechanical clocks were probably built in the monasteries. Although no one knows when or where they were invented, several monasteries and cathedrals appear to have had mechanical clocks by the end of the thirteenth **century.**

The first mechanical clocks were big and heavy. They contained metal cogs, which were turned by a weight and a bell. They also contained a mechanism called an **escapement** that controlled the rate at which the cogs turned.

The clocks were poor timekeepers. At best, they could keep the right time to within about a quarter of an hour each day. Unlike a modern clock, they had no face or hands. They told the time by ringing a bell every hour. The first clocks to have hands usually had only an hour hand. Minute hands became common in the mid-seventeenth century when the accuracy of clocks improved with the introduction of the **pendulum**.

The escape wheel turns by one tooth's worth for every "back and forth" swing of the foliot. As it turns, other cogs in the clock, which are not shown in the diagram, turn slightly too.

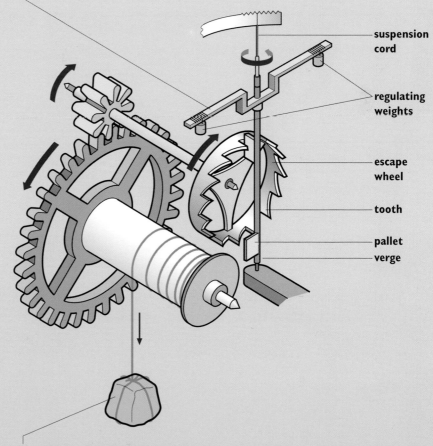

The foliot swings from side to side and controls the rate at which the clock ticks.

suspension cord

regulating weights

escape wheel

tooth

pallet

verge

The weight makes the cogs turn and the verge and foliot swing from side to side.

13

Interval Timers

A candle can be used as an interval timer. The time when it is lit must be known if it is used as a timekeeper.

Fire, sand, and water

Although **sundials** could be used for telling the time of day when it was sunny, they couldn't be used inside a building or for measuring short time intervals. The first mechanical clocks weren't useful for measuring short time intervals either.

Over the years, many different types of interval timers have been designed. Many timers made use of fire, sand, or water. Some of them are shown here. A good timer is one that is easy to use and always gives the same results.

This water timer was made in about 1670. It works like a sandglass. When the timer is turned, the decorative cap is removed. It takes thirty minutes for the water to run from the top to the bottom.

In this Chinese fire clock, a stick of burning incense burns through the threads one by one. This allows the weights to fall onto a metal tray with a "clang."

Sandglasses

Sandglasses were invented in the fourteenth **century.** They were used in many different places. Law courts and churches used sandglasses to make sure that people did not speak too long.

Doctors used them to measure pulse rates, and sailors used them to estimate their speed by measuring how far they had gone in a specific time. Sailors also used them to time the watches—the period when a sailor was on duty. Sailors keeping watch at night would sometimes "flog the glass." In other words, they would turn the sandglass early so they could finish their watches early, too! Cooks also used sand timers. They can still be bought today.

This teacher is using a sandglass in the fourteenth century.

This sandglass is over 350 years old. It takes the sand one hour to run from the top container to the bottom one.

This modern sandglass was designed for classroom use. It takes the sand one minute to run from the top container to the bottom one.

15

Better Timekeepers
and Portable Timekeepers

pendulum

weight

This clock was built in the 1660s. Like many other old clocks, it has been modified and no longer has its original **escapement**.

Clocks use energy

Clocks need a source of energy to make their cogs and hands turn and their bells ring. In the earliest clocks, energy came from a slowly falling weight. Even when these clocks got smaller and lighter, the weight prevented them from being moved while they were still running. It also prevented them from being placed on top of a table or cupboard.

In the late fifteenth **century,** clockmakers began to use the energy stored in a coiled spring to drive some of their clocks. Unlike weight-driven clocks, spring-driven ones could be placed almost anywhere.

Pendulum clocks

A **pendulum** will swing from side to side at a steadier rate than the **foliot** did in the earliest clocks. The first successful pendulum clock was designed by Christiaan Huygens in 1656. Built by Salomon Coster, it was completed in 1657. It was far more accurate than any timekeeper that had ever been built.

Clocks that were designed to be moved frequently had big handles on top of their cases. The carrying case next to this spring-driven clock is covered with leather.

The anchor escapement shown here was an improvement on the verge escapement used by Huygens in the first pendulum clock. As the pendulum swings back and forth, the escape wheel is allowed to turn in a series of steps or ticks. As it turns, the hands and other cogs in the clock (not shown here) turn slightly too.

anchor escapement

escape wheel

driving weight

pendulum

Unlike most earlier clocks, it was fitted with both a minute hand and an hour hand. Over the years, the accuracy of the best available pendulum clocks improved from about ten seconds a day to one second a year.

This French watch is about 350 years old. Like most other clocks and watches of its age, it was made without a minute hand. The chain is called a *chatelaine*. The winding key and two seals (for sealing letters) are attached to it.

Wrist watches

The first wrist watches were made in the late 1800s and became much more common during World War I. Most watches made until the 1970s were spring driven and regulated by the **oscillations** of a **balance wheel** and balance spring. Most modern watches are electrically driven by a battery and regulated by the oscillations taking place inside a **quartz** crystal.

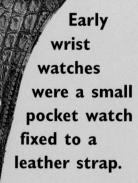

Early wrist watches were a small pocket watch fixed to a leather strap.

Finding Time

One turn later: The Earth needs to rotate through about 1° more to bring the person back to midday (square on to the Sun).

The earth turns through about 361° from one midday to the next. This means that it rotates on its axis 366¼ times during the course of a 365¼ day year.

Between **midday** today and midday tomorrow, when the sun crosses the same **meridian**, the earth will have turned on its **axis** through an angle of about 361 degrees (361°). The earth has to turn through about one degree more than one full turn (360°) to take us from one midday to the next because it is also moving around the sun.

Some days are longer than others

The earth's **orbit** is slightly elliptical, or oval in shape. The earth is closest to the sun in January and farthest from the sun in July. As the earth gets closer to the sun, it travels more quickly in its orbit. When this happens, it has to turn a very tiny amount farther on its axis from one midday to the next. This means that each natural or **solar day** varies slightly in length throughout the year.

Sidereal days are always the same length

Unlike the sun, a star will cross the same meridian line each time the earth spins exactly once on its axis. By observing the stars with a telescope pointing along the meridian, astronomers are able to more accurately record the moment that each star crosses from one side to the other. The time it takes for the earth to turn through 360° on its axis is always the same and is called a **sidereal day.** A sidereal day is about four minutes shorter than the average length of a solar day or **mean solar day.**

meridian line

The telescope can be moved up and down, but not from side to side. Each turn of the earth brings the same star back into view. Telescopes like this are called **transit telescopes.** Most observatories had one. One of their uses was to check the accuracy of the observatory's main sidereal clock. The sidereal clock was then used to check other clocks. All the clocks could be checked because mean solar time can be calculated from sidereal time.

Finding the time with a telescope

Individual stars always cross a particular meridian at the same sidereal time each day. Because of this, the time can be found far more accurately through regular observation than with a **sundial** or from observations of the sun. The telescope is similar to a clock hand sweeping across the sky as the earth spins on its axis. The stars are similar to the numbers on a dial. **Observatories** had some clocks set to show mean solar time, which is what ordinary people's clocks would have shown, and others that looked the same but ticked slightly faster, which were set to show sidereal time.

This transit telescope was the ultimate source of **Greenwich Mean Time** from 1816 to 1850.

Local Time

and Greenwich Mean Time

Local apparent time

The farther west you are, the later the sun rises and the later it sets. When a **sundial** in Boston, Massachusetts, shows 12:00 noon, farther west in Utica, New York, one will show 11:44 A.M. The time shown by a sundial is the **local apparent time**.

Mean time

At the beginning of the nineteenth **century,** anyone lucky enough to own a clock or a watch would probably have set it to their own **local time**. It would have shown local mean solar time, more commonly known as local **mean time**. Local mean time is sometimes ahead of local apparent time and sometimes behind it. The local mean time at Greenwich in London, England, is called **Greenwich Mean Time**.

This pocket watch was made in the mid-1800s. It has two-minute hands. One would have been set to Greenwich Mean Time and the other to the user's own local time.

Standard time

In the days before the railroads, when local time was still in common use, a journey from Boston to Utica would probably have taken several days. Each time travelers stopped at an inn, they would reset their watches to a slightly earlier time. By the time they reached Utica, their watches would be set sixteen minutes earlier than the clocks in Boston.

Railroads allowed journeys like these to be made more quickly by more people. Imagine three passengers on a train to Plymouth, England: one got on in London; one got on in Reading, about forty miles to the west; and one got on in Exeter, about 160 miles farther to the west. If each passenger had set a watch to his or her own local time, what would each watch show when the train arrived at Plymouth at 3:00 in the afternoon **local time**? The London passenger's watch would show 3:16. The Reading passenger's watch would show 3:12. And the Exeter passenger's watch would show 3:02. You can probably imagine how confusing things could get, especially when figuring out the train schedules!

In the United States, the difference in local time between New York City on the East Coast and San Francisco on the West Coast is over three and a quarter hours. The problem was solved in 1883 when four different **time zones,** each with its own **standard time,** were set up.

The railroad companies in other countries faced similar problems. The British railway companies solved their problem by using **Greenwich Mean Time** at their stations, rather than local time. Years later, in 1880, the British Government decided that Greenwich Mean Time should become the standard time used by everyone in the British Isles.

Norwich ●
sundial 5 minutes ahead of one in London

Reading ●

● **London**
sundial 16 minutes ahead of one in Plymouth

Exeter ●

● **Plymouth**

N
W — E
S

A sundial or clock set to local time in London will show an earlier time than one in Norwich to the east, but a later time than one in Plymouth to the west.

What's the Time?

The time ball at the Greenwich Observatory was installed in 1833. The ball drops from the top of the mast at one o'clock in the afternoon each day. It was used by sailors on the nearby Thames River to set their **chronometers** before setting out across the oceans.

Time signals

When we want to know the time, we normally look at a watch or a clock. You may have noticed though, that different people's watches often say slightly different times. So how do we know what the time really is? One way we can find out is from the television or radio. Most radio announcers tell their listeners the time at frequent intervals. They usually say something like, "The time is now twenty-eight minutes past eight." The trouble is, this takes a few seconds to say and the listener can't be sure of exactly when it was twenty-eight minutes past eight. Was it as the announcer began to speak, when they finished, or somewhere in between?

As a result, some radio stations transmit a special time signal. At certain times of the day, usually on the hour, a small number of beeps are broadcast in quick succession. The first beeps are a warning to get ready and the last beep is the one to set your watch by. In France, these time signals consist of three beeps, and in the United Kingdom, they consist of six. The first British time signal ever to be transmitted came from the Royal **Observatory** at Greenwich—the home of **Greenwich Mean Time**. Some clocks contain a radio receiver and automatically adjust themselves to the correct time.

The speaking clock

Some people can telephone a speaking clock. The first speaking clock was set up in France in 1905. The British speaking clock was set up in 1936. It gives the time every ten seconds.

What happened before time signals?

Before television and radio, it was much harder for people to check their clocks and watches. Most people had to rely on a **sundial** or another clock that had been checked with a sundial.

The time ball at the Sydney Observatory in Australia was installed in 1858. The mechanism was made in London.

This clock outside the Greenwich Observatory was installed for public use in 1852. The hour hand goes around once each day, so the time shown is a few seconds before 9:07 A.M. The clock is controlled by a master clock, which sends electrical signals once each second to make it tick at the correct rate. People still use it to check their watches.

Longitude and Time

Latitude and longitude

Lines of **latitude** mark how far north or south you are. Lines of **longitude** mark how far east or west you are. Unlike latitude, which is measured from the **equator**, there is no obvious point from which to measure longitude. Until 1884, it was measured from many different places, including Greenwich; Paris, France; and Lisbon, Portugal. After 1884, there was officially only one place—the **meridian** line running through the Royal **Observatory** at Greenwich.

Where am I?

When Christopher Columbus sailed across the Atlantic Ocean in 1492, there was no way to measure a ship's longitude when land was out of sight. Most of the world remained unexplored and the sea charts, or maps, were inaccurate and incomplete. Later, as the trade routes opened up, these problems became more and more important. Journeys often took longer than expected and could end in disaster

Shipwrecks would often result in the loss of life and cargo, as well as the loss of the ship.

if a ship got lost and ran aground. As a result, large rewards were offered to anyone who could find a practical way of measuring longitude at sea. Two solutions were both linked to the measurement of time.

Longitude is linked to time

When it is **midday** on one side of the earth, it is midnight on the other. Each 15° of longitude is equivalent to a time difference of one hour. To find how far east or west they had sailed, sailors needed to find out both the **local time**—which could be done from observations of the positions of the sun or the stars—and the time back home at exactly the same moment.

Finding the time back home

How, though, was a sailor supposed to find out what the time was back home? One suggestion was to take a clock to sea that was set to show the time back home. However, clocks in 1600 were not accurate enough to be reliable at sea. The more accurate **pendulum** clocks, invented in 1656, would not work because the pendulum would swing at different speeds with the rocking of the boat. In the sixteenth and seventeenth **centuries,** most people thought that an accurate seagoing clock could never be built. They looked for solutions elsewhere.

North Pole

Greenwich (London)

Prime Meridian

27°

74°

90°

45°

Equator

15°W

0°

15°E

20°N

10°N

10°S

20°S

The latitude of this ship is 27° north. Its longitude is 74° west. Its latitude could have been found either from measurements of the height of the midday sun or from the height of the Pole Star. The time difference (local time) from Greenwich is 4 hours, 56 minutes.

ongitude
rs time difference)

180° of longitude
(12 hours time difference)

6 pm

9 pm

3 pm

light from
the sun

night

12 midday

3 am

9 am

6 am

longitude
r time difference)

longitude and time

The *Nautical Almanac*—
One Solution to the Longitude Problem

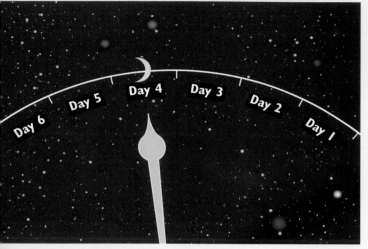

Tick-tock moon clock

Longitude can be measured with the help of the moon. At the same time the earth is rotating on its **axis**, the moon is **orbiting** it in the same direction. This makes the moon appear to move across the sky from east to west at a slightly slower rate than the stars. As the night goes on, the moon slowly moves across the background of stars like a hand moving across the face of a clock.

The moon appears to move against the background of stars and can be used as a clock to find the time at Greenwich. The moon (the hand) takes 27½ days to go around the dial (the stars) once. Sailors were only able to read the moon clock with the help of the *Nautical Almanac*.

Unfortunately, the moon clock can only be read with the help of tables listing where the moon will be seen at different times on different days of the year. The Royal **Observatory** at Greenwich produced the first set of tables for use by sailors in 1766. They listed where the moon would be seen at different times from Greenwich for the following three years. The book containing the tables was called the *Nautical Almanac.*

A page from the first *Nautical Almanac.* The almanac was produced with the help of lunar tables provided by the German astronomer Tobias Mayer.

Using the *Nautical Almanac*

To find their longitude, sailors had to measure three angles: the angle up to the moon, the angle up to a nearby bright star, and the angle between them. After several long calculations, sailors would then be able to read off the time at Greenwich from the *Nautical Almanac.* Provided the sailors had also found their own **local time**, they would then be able to calculate the time difference from Greenwich. All that had to be done then was to turn the time difference into a longitude difference with each hour of time representing fifteen degrees (15°) of longitude.

This method of measuring longitude is called the lunar distance method. It turned out to be very reliable and was used by many ocean-going sailors from around 1780 until well into the 1800s. The publication of the first *Nautical Almanac* began the chain of events that led to Greenwich becoming the home of the **Prime Meridian** and the center of time in 1884.

Having measured these three angles, a sailor could then use the *Nautical Almanac* to find the time at Greenwich and thus the longitude.

A room at the Greenwich Observatory in 1676. The Observatory was founded in 1675 by King Charles II of England to help solve the longitude problem. The two clocks to the left of the door were used to check that the earth spins on its axis at a steady rate.

Harrison's Seagoing Clocks—
A Second Solution to the Longitude Problem

The fabulous longitude prize

In 1714, the British Government set up the Board of **Longitude**. The Board of Longitude offered a large reward or prize to anyone who could find a way to measure longitude to the nearest half of a degree.

Could a clock win?

John Harrison, a carpenter and self-taught clockmaker, heard about the prize and decided to try to win it. He knew that to win the prize, any clock he built would have to gain or lose no more than 2.8 seconds a day while at sea. He

H1

designed a completely new type of clock without a **pendulum** so that it would not be affected by the tossing of a boat. The clock is now known as H1. When it was tested at sea in 1736, it performed far better than any clock that had ever been at sea before—but it wasn't good enough to win the longitude prize.

H2

John Harrison finally wins the prize

Harrison was given money to develop a modified design. By the time H2 was finished two years later, Harrison realized that this clock, too, would not win the prize.

H3

Without even having it tested at sea, he set to work on a third clock, H3. He worked on H3 for the next nineteen years, but he knew in the end that it would not work well enough. While still working on H3, Harrison decided to try out a different design. The clock that he built, H4, looks like a giant pocket watch. It was tested at sea in 1761.

H4

Although Harrison thought that H4 had performed well enough to win the prize, the Board of Longitude wasn't happy with the fairness of the test and refused to award him the full prize. They demanded that further tests be carried out and that copies of H4 be made. Many years later, Harrison was finally rewarded, but only after King George III became involved. By then, it was 1773 and Harrison was 80 years old.

A copy of H4 was taken by Captain James Cook on his second voyage to the Pacific Ocean in 1772. He described it as, "Our never failing guide," and used it to construct some of the first charts of Australia and New Zealand. Many people now consider H4 to be the most important clock ever made. It lead to the development of more accurate watches and other seagoing clocks or **chronometers**.

John Harrison. H4 is on the table and H3 is behind it. H3 is similar in size to H1 and H2.

The Prime Meridian
and the Universal Day

In the early 1880s, sailors measured east and west from several different places. The main meridians used are shown here.

East and west from where?

The end of the 1760s marked a turning point in navigation. After years of being unable to measure their **longitude** at sea, sailors now had two ways to measure it. Both ways worked by measuring time differences. Although a **chronometer** would allow the difference in time from any chosen town or city to be measured directly, this was not the case with the lunar distance method. The ***Nautical Almanac*** only gave the time on the **meridian** that ran through the Royal **Observatory** at Greenwich. Not everyone chose to measure longitude at sea from the Greenwich meridian. The French and Algerians for example, measured it from the Paris meridian, while the Swedes measured it from the Stockholm meridian.

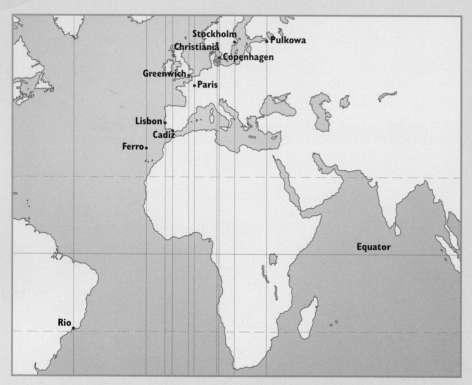

Choosing a Prime Meridian

By the early 1880s, many countries could see the advantages of measuring east and west from just one meridian. As a result, the International Meridian Conference took place in Washington, D.C., in 1884.

The meridian line running through the eyepiece of the **transit telescope** at Greenwich was chosen as the **Prime Meridian** of the world. There were several reasons why the Greenwich meridian was chosen. The main reason is that nearly two-thirds of the world's ships were already using it.

Universal Time and the Universal Day

The conference also decided to create a single time system for the whole world. Until then, time had always been measured from different starting points according to where a person was in the world. For example, the day in London began after the day in Sydney, Australia, but before the day in New York. The Universal Day gave people an easy way to measure time from the same starting point, no matter where on the earth's surface they were.

The Prime Meridian begins in the eyepiece of this transit telescope at the Royal Observatory in Greenwich. The telescope was the source of Greenwich Mean Time from 1851 until 1927.

It was decided that each Universal Day would start for the whole world at the moment it reached midnight on the Greenwich meridian. **Greenwich Mean Time,** therefore, became the official time for the world. Since 1928, it has also been known as **Universal Time** (UT). Following the International Meridian Conference, agreement was reached for setting up our present system of **time zones**.

The Prime Meridian outside the observatory buildings at Greenwich.

Time Zones

Greenwich—the center of time

After the International **Meridian** Conference of 1884, more and more countries began to use **standard time** instead of **local time**. Some large countries, such as Australia and Russia, were divided into many **time zones**. Other large countries, such as China and India, used the same standard time for the whole country.

The **Prime Meridian** and **Greenwich Mean Time** became the center of the time zone system. Countries to the east usually used standard times a whole number of hours ahead of Greenwich Mean Time. Those to the west normally used standard times that were a whole number of hours behind.

The world's countries fit loosely into a grid of twenty-four time zones—each 15° of longitude "wide."

Greenwich

Prime Meridian

Lagos

New York

Rio de Janeiro

Summer time

Some countries, for example the United States and France, switch to **daylight savings time** for part of the year. This is done by setting clocks forward by an hour in the spring and setting them back again in the fall.

The switch is made to make better use of daylight hours. For example, instead of getting light at five o'clock in the morning, while most people are still in bed, and then dark at seven o'clock in the evening, it gets light at six o'clock in the morning and dark at eight o'clock in the evening.

The International Date Line

The *Victoria* was the first ship to sail around the world. It was the only ship from Portuguese explorer Ferdinand Magellan's fleet of five ships to circle the earth. Magellan's fleet left Spain and sailed in a western direction on September 20, 1519. Almost three years later, before reaching home, the *Victoria* stopped for supplies at the Cape Verde Islands. The crew was surprised that it was Thursday, July 10, 1522. They thought the date was Wednesday, July 9, 1522.

Something similar would happen if a person was to set off around the world in a western direction and turn his or her watch back by an hour each time a new time zone was entered. By the time the person returned home, his or her watch would show a time that was 24 hours behind everybody else's time.

To prevent things like this from happening to travelers, an imaginary line known as the **International Date Line** has been created on the opposite side of the world from Greenwich. When travelers cross the date line, they must adjust the date on their watches. The direction in which the adjustment is made depends on whether they are traveling from east to west or from west to east.

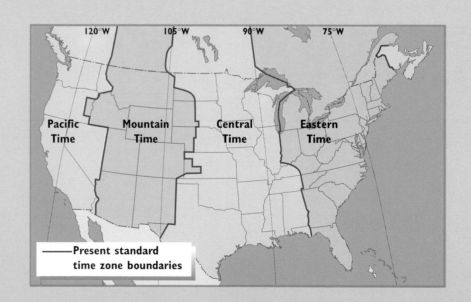

North America's time zones.

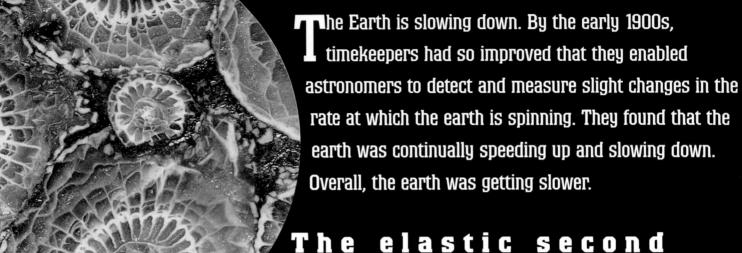

The Earth is slowing down. By the early 1900s, timekeepers had so improved that they enabled astronomers to detect and measure slight changes in the rate at which the earth is spinning. They found that the earth was continually speeding up and slowing down. Overall, the earth was getting slower.

The elastic second

Although the changes were far too small to bother most people, they puzzled astronomers and scientists. If the rate at which the earth was spinning kept changing, then the exact length of a second would keep changing too. Eventually in 1956, astronomers and scientists determined the exact length of a second. The length they chose was equal to the average length the second had in 1900.

The fixed second

Meanwhile, a group of scientists had been developing **atomic clocks**. These clocks were much more accurate than the best **pendulum** clocks. So in 1967, without changing the length of a second, scientists changed its definition to one based on **atomic time**.

Without any adjustment, the time shown by atomic clocks would eventually get more and more out of step with the movement of the sun across the sky.

By studying the daily growth bands of fossil corals, which vary with the seasons, scientists have discovered that four hundred million years ago, there were more days in a year. The earth took only twenty-two of our present hours to spin around once on its axis.

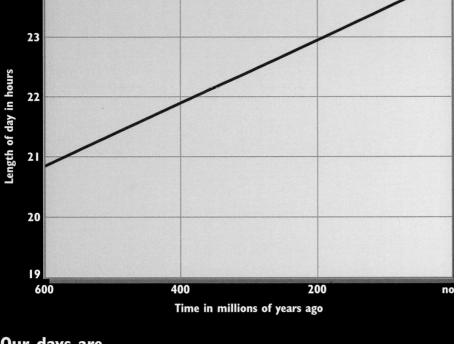

Length of day in hours

600 400 200 now

Time in millions of years ago

This is because the clocks tick at a steady rate even though the earth is slowing down. In a few thousand years, unadjusted atomic clocks would show 12:00 noon, even though people were just waking up in the morning. To prevent this problem, our present system of adding or subtracting **leap seconds** was started.

Our days are gradually getting longer.

Coordinated Universal Time

Atomic time that has been adjusted by the addition or subtraction of leap seconds is called Coordinated Universal Time (UTC). The time shown by most clocks around the world today is based on it.

The adjustments are made so that Coordinated Universal Time never differs from **Greenwich Mean Time** by more than 0.9 seconds. Between 1972 and the beginning of 1999, a total of twenty-two leap seconds were added. Leap seconds are normally only added or subtracted at the end (midnight UTC) of the last day of June or the last day of December.

Timekeepers:
More Accurate than the Earth

A tiny computer chip inside the watch makes the quartz crystal vibrate. It also counts the vibrations and as a result, produces one electrical impulse each second. This is fed to a motor that turns the hands.

battery

The slice of quartz crystal is enclosed inside this protective casing.

Clocks count oscillations

Clocks work by counting vibrations or **oscillations,** for example, the swings of a **pendulum**. The minute hand of a clock with a pendulum that takes 1 second to swing from side to side will turn through one-tenth of a degree with every swing and through 360 degrees with every 3,600 swings. The clock will count 86,400 swings of the pendulum each day and 604,800 swings each week.

Quartz clocks

In the same way that an oscillating pendulum was found to swing more regularly than the oscillating **foliot** used in the earliest clocks, a slice of vibrating **quartz** crystal oscillates more regularly than a pendulum. The tiny piece of quartz crystal buried inside a clock or watch vibrates or oscillates tens of thousands of times each second. This is so fast that to the naked eye, it wouldn't appear to be vibrating at all.

If you have a quartz watch or clock, it almost certainly keeps time to better than one second a day, something that only **chronometers** and the most expensive pendulum clocks could do at the end of the nineteenth **century**. Specially engineered quartz clocks are able to keep time thousands of times more accurately than the ones you have at home.

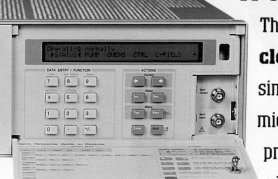

Atomic clocks

The world's most accurate clocks are **atomic clocks**. They make use of microwaves similar to those used by cellular phones and microwave ovens. The microwaves are produced inside the clock by an oscillator vibrating 9,192,631,770 times a second.

Unlike the earth, which is losing around I second a year, this atomic clock will lose or gain no more than I second in the next 1,600,000 years—if it runs for that long! The exact time today comes from the averaged readings of more than 200 atomic clocks located around the world.

When a beam of **cesium** atoms is bombarded with the microwaves, the atoms absorb the wave energy and change their magnetic properties. The cesium atoms are used to help adjust the rate of the oscillator to exactly 9,192,631,770 vibrations a second because they will only absorb microwaves at this frequency. An electronic device then counts the vibrations and converts the count rate into a time on a clock face.

In 1967, scientists redefined the second as the period equal to the duration of 9,192,631,770 of these vibrations. So every time 9,192,631,770 vibrations are counted, the time shown by the digital display increases by one second.

Modern communication systems depend on the split-second timing provided by atomic clocks.

Months and Years

We see the moon, because it reflects light from the sun. The side of the moon facing the sun is always lit up. When the moon is at **A,** between the earth and the sun, the whole lit side is facing away from the earth. None of the moon can be seen. This is a new moon. About two weeks later, when the moon is on the opposite side of the earth at **E,** all of the lit face can be seen. This is a full moon.

The phases of the moon

The appearance of the moon changes in a regular pattern as it **orbits** the earth. Many of our ancestors created their calendars around these changes or phases. The length of our months is based on the length of time between one new moon and the next. A new moon occurs when the moon passes in its orbit between the earth and the sun.

Synodic months

At the same time the moon is going around the earth, the earth is going around the sun. Therefore, the moon has to complete slightly more than one full orbit of the earth from one new moon to the next. It takes just over 29 ½ days for it to do this. This length of time is known as a **synodic month.** In the time that the earth takes to orbit the sun once, there are twelve synodic months with about eleven extra days left over.

Position	Appearance of Moon	
	view from near the North Pole	view from near the South Pole
A new moon	Moon not visible	Moon not visible
B		
C first quarter		
D		
E full moon		
F		
G last quarter		
H		

Earth

Light from the Sun

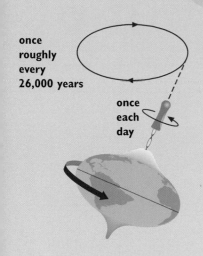

once
roughly
every
26,000 years

once
each
day

The earth spinning on its axis is a bit like a spinning top whose handle traces out a circle as it spins. This is called precession. It takes about 26,000 years for the earth's axis or "handle" to trace out one full circle. About 13,000 years from now, the earth's axis will be leaning in completely the opposite direction compared with today.

The tropical year

Although the direction in which its **axis** is leaning hardly changes from year to year, as the earth orbits the sun, the change becomes noticeable over a period of hundreds or thousands of years. To make sure that winter in the northern hemisphere always begins in December, our present calendar automatically takes the small yearly change in the direction of the earth's axis into account. It is based on a period of time called the **tropical year,** which is about twenty minutes less than the time it takes for the earth to orbit the sun exactly once. There are a fraction under 365¼ **mean solar days** in a tropical year.

So, just as there aren't exactly twelve synodic months in a year, there aren't exactly 365 days either. Different societies and religions dealt with these problems in different ways and developed different calendars.

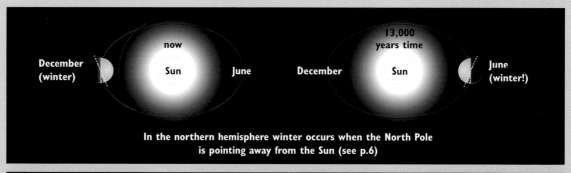

In the northern hemisphere winter occurs when the North Pole is pointing away from the Sun (see p.6)

The upper diagram shows what would happen if our year was based on the 365.256 days it takes for the earth to go around the sun. The length of our year (365.242 days) has been chosen so that it is always winter in the northern hemisphere in December.

The Gregorian Calendar

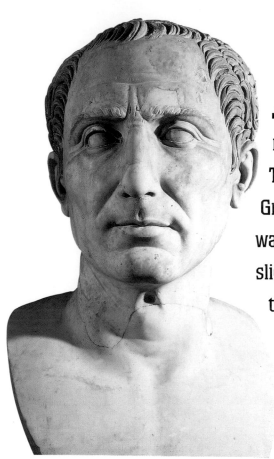

Julius Caesar began our system of leap years more than 2,000 years ago.

Although many people were still using different calendars for religious purposes, by the start of the twentieth **century,** most people across the world used the **Gregorian Calendar.** This is the calendar that nearly everyone uses today. The Gregorian Calendar developed from the Roman Calendar and first was used in 1582. Except for February, all of the months ended up slightly longer than a **synodic month** of 29½ days. As a result, the first day of each month does not stay in step with the appearance of a new crescent moon.

The Julian Calendar

In the year 46 **B.C.**, the Roman dictator Julius Caesar changed the Roman Calendar. He began the system of **leap years** with every fourth year having 366 days instead of 365. The leap years are those whose year number is divisible by four. The calendar he devised is known as the Julian Calendar.

Caesar's rule about leap years didn't quite work though. For it to work perfectly, the **tropical year** would have had to be exactly 365¼ days long. At a fraction under 365¼ days it was, of course, slightly too short. The eleven minute error in the length of the year slowly began to add up, and as the years went by, the months and the seasons became out of step. According to the calendar, by 1582 the first day of spring occurred ten days too early on March 11 instead of on March 21 in the northern hemisphere.

The Gregorian Calendar

Pope Gregory XIII, after whom the Gregorian Calendar is named, made two changes to the Julian Calendar. First, he advanced it by ten days so that the day following October 4, 1582 was not October 5 but October 15. Second, a slight change was made to the rule about leap years. The new rules stated that instead of every fourth year being a leap year, the years whose year number ends in *00*, which are divisible by four, would only be leap years if they were also divisible by four hundred. So although the year 2000 will be a leap year, the year 2100 will not.

Pope Gregory XIII changed the rules about leap years in 1582.

In this painting by William Hogarth, the injured man has his foot on a poster that says, "Give us our eleven days."

Although most Catholic countries quickly made the change, nonCatholic countries were not too happy at first. The British, who were Protestants, resisted for more than 150 years. By the time the British switched to the Gregorian Calendar in 1752, the calendar was eleven days off with the seasons. When September 14 immediately followed September 2, there were riots on the streets of London, with people shouting, "Give us back our eleven days!"

The Jewish and the Islamic
Calendars

The beginning of each Jewish and Islamic month coincides with the appearance of a thin crescent moon in the sky.

The new moon

The length of each Jewish and Islamic month is closely linked to the **synodic month** of 29 days, 12 hours, and 44 minutes, or just over 29½ days. The first day of each month normally occurs with the appearance of a new crescent moon in the sky. Each new day begins at sunset.

The Islamic Calendar

The Islamic year has twelve months consisting alternately of 30 and 29 days, or an average of 29½ days, making 354 days altogether. The average length of each month is about forty-four minutes less than the actual length of a synodic month. These forty-four minute blocks of time add up month by month, totaling just under nine hours in a year. If the calendar wasn't adjusted to allow for this, the new crescent moon would appear later and later each month through the years. To prevent this from happening, about every third year has an extra day inserted at the end of the twelfth month, making it 30 instead of 29 days long.

Each Islamic year is about eleven days shorter than the **tropical year** on which the **Gregorian Calendar** is based. Unlike the Gregorian Calendar, the Islamic Calendar does not stay in step with the seasons.

Muharram	(30 days)
Safar	(29 days)
Rabi I	(30 days)
Rabi II	(29 days)
Jumada I	(30 days)
Jumada II	(29 days)
Rajab	(30 days)
Shaban	(29 days)
Ramadan	(30 days)
Shawwal	(29 days)
Dhu al-Qadah	(30 days)
Dhu al-Hijjah	(29 or 30 days)

The twelve months of the Islamic year. The ninth month, Ramadan, is the fasting month.

The Islamic new year sometimes falls in the summer, sometimes in the spring, sometimes in the winter, and sometimes in the fall. According to the Gregorian Calendar, each Islamic year begins around eleven days earlier than the one before.

The Jewish Calendar

The Jewish Calendar is more complex. It, too, has months consisting alternately of 30 and 29 days. Some years have 12 months like the Islamic Calendar, but other years have 13. On this basis, a 12-month year would consist of 354 days, about 11 days less than a tropical year of about 365¼ days. A 13-month year would consist of 384 days, about 19 days more than a tropical year. To make the average length 365 days, 12 out of every 19 years have 12 months, and the other 7 years have 13 months.

In some years, the calendar is adjusted by adding or subtracting a day. As a result, years of 12 months can have either 353, 354, or 355 days. Years of 13 months can have 383, 384, or 385 days. Unlike the Islamic Calendar, the Jewish Calendar keeps more or less in step with the seasons.

Tishri	(30 days)
Heshvan	(29 or 30 days)
Kislev	(29 or 30 days)
Tevet	(29 days)
Shevat	(30 days)
Adar	(29 or 30 days)
Nisan	(30 days)
Iyar	(29 days)
Sivan	(30 days)
Tammuz	(29 days)
Av	(30 days)
Elul	(29 days)

The twelve months of the Jewish year. In some years, a thirteenth month, Adar Sheni, is added after Adar.

Centuries and Millenniums

The decision to count years from the birth of Christ was made over 500 years after he was born. The Catholic monk Dionysius Exiguus, also known as Dennis the Short, figured out that Jesus had been born on December 25 in the Roman year 753 **AUC**— counting from the founding of the city of Rome. He therefore renamed January 1, 754 AUC as January 1, A.D.1. Many scholars now believe that Jesus was born a few years earlier.

Counting years

For many people, the beginning of a new **century** or **millennium** is a time for special celebrations. The different calendars in use count their years from different starting points. These usually coincided with an event that was particularly important to the religion or society. The Ancient Egyptians began at year one whenever a new pharaoh was crowned, so no one ever celebrated the start of a new century, let alone a new millennium.

Counting forward and backward

The starting point for the **Gregorian Calendar** is Jesus Christ's birth. **B.C.** stands for *before Christ* and is used when years are counted backwards from Christ's birth, for example, 46 B.C. Some people prefer to use BCE instead. It stands for *before the common era*. **A.D.** stands for *anno Domini*, which means "in the year of our Lord." It is used to make it clear that the year referred to has been counted from Christ's birth. Some people prefer to use C.E., which stands for *common era* instead. The date July 16, A.D. 622, coincides with the beginning of year one of the Islamic Calendar, which began when the prophet Muhammad escaped from his enemies in Mecca.

On January 1, 1998, the Eiffel Tower in Paris, France, shows 730 days before the start of the year 2000.

A new millennium

The first century A.D. began at the start of year 1. The second century A.D. began at the start of the year 101. In the same way, the twentieth century began at the start of the year 1901. The start of the Universal Day on January 1, 1901—when it was midnight on the **Prime Meridian** at Greenwich—marked the exact moment that the twentieth century officially began.

Although the twenty-first century and third millennium will begin at the start of January 1, 2001, most of the world will celebrate a year early at the start of the year 2000. Greenwich will be at the center of these celebrations. The year A.D. 2000 begins in the fourth month of the Jewish year 5760 and the ninth month of the Islamic year 1420.

The countdown clock on the Prime Meridian at the Greenwich **observatory** shows 932 days until the start of the year 2000.

At the end of 1999, many computers will reset their calendars to the year 1900 or 1980. This problem is known as the millennium bug. It will occur because of the way the computers have been programmed. Many people are concerned about the effect it might have on computers used in transportation systems, hospital equipment, and businesses.

45

Glossary

A.D. Stands for *anno Domini,* which means "in the year of our Lord" in the Latin language. It is normally used with a year number to indicate how long after Christ's birth an event occurred. It is also called CE (Common Era).

A.M. stands for *ante meridiem* and means a time that occurs in the morning before 12:00 noon

atomic clock most accurate type of clock, losing or gaining no more than one second in 10 million years

atomic time time that is kept by an atomic clock

AUC Stands for *Ab Urbe Condita.* The term was used by the Romans with a year number to indicate how long after the founding of the city of Rome an event occurred.

axis imaginary line running through the center of the earth between the North and the South Poles, around which the earth spins; any line around which an object spins

balance wheel oscillating wheel used with a balance spring in some clocks and watches to make them tick at the right rate

B.C. Stands for "before Christ." It is normally used with a year number to indicate how long before Christ's birth an event occurred. It is also called BCE, or "Before the Common Era."

century period of one hundred years

cesium soft, silvery metal whose atomic properties enable extremely accurate atomic clocks to work

chronometer portable clock that is able to keep accurate time, usually at sea, and normally set to **Greenwich Mean Time** wherever on the earth's surface it is being used

daylight savings time standard time used in some countries during the summer months to make better use of the hours of daylight, done by setting clocks one hour ahead of the standard time used for the rest of the year.

equator imaginary line around the center of the earth that separates the northern and southern hemispheres

escapement device that makes a clock mechanism turn with a series of stop-start movements or ticks

foliot swinging bar used by the first clockmakers to make their clocks tick at the right rate

Gregorian Calendar name given to the Julian Calendar after it had been changed by Pope Gregory XIII in 1582, now used by my most people around the world

Greenwich Mean Time (GMT) local mean time at Greenwich, England, and the standard time originally used by the whole United Kingdom

International Date Line imaginary line that runs through the Pacific Ocean, upon which passing, travelers heading west must set their watches forward by a day, while those going east set them back by a day

latitude measure of how far north or south of the equator something is

leap second second that is occasionally added to clocks to ensure that they stay in step with the spinning, but generally slowing, earth

leap year year with 366 days rather than the usual 365 days, usually happening every four years

local apparent time time shown by a **sundial**

local time time linked to the position of the sun in the sky.
longitude measure of how far east or west of the **Prime Meridian** at Greenwich, England

mean solar day average length of a solar day, equal in time to twenty-four hours

mean time time measurement based on the **mean solar day** of twenty-four hours

meridian any north-south line, either imaginary or real, on the earth's surface

midday time when the sun reaches its highest point of the day, crossing from the east side of the **meridian** to the west

millennium period of one thousand years

observatory building from which astronomers make observations of stars and planets with telescopes and other instruments

orbit path of a planet around the sun or the moon around the earth

oscillation side-to-side movement of a vibrating or swinging object, for example a **pendulum**

pendulum swinging wooden or metal rod with a weight attached to its lower end used in some clocks to make them tick at the correct rate

P.M. stands for *post meridiem* and means a time that occurs in the afternoon or evening after 12:00 noon

Prime Meridian the north-south line running from the North Pole to the South Pole through the observatory at Greenwich, and the line from which east and west are now measured

quartz crystalline mineral found in many types of rocks that can be made to **oscillate,** used in some clocks to make them tick at the right rate

sidereal day time it takes for the earth to spin around once on its **axis,** equal to about 4 minutes less than a **mean solar day**

sidereal year time it takes for the earth to go around the sun once, equal in time to 365.256 days

solar day period of time between one **midday** (or midnight) and the next

standard time agreed upon time to which all clocks in a country or part of a country are set

sundial device that uses shadows to find the time from the sun's position in the sky

synodic month period of time between one new moon and the next, equal in time to about 29 1/2 days

temperate zones two regions of the earth between the **tropics** and the polar zones

time zone one of the twenty-four divisions of the earth's surface, in which clocks are set to the same **standard time**—normally a whole number of hours ahead of or behind Coordinated Universal Time.

transit telescope telescope mounted on its own **meridian** so that it can swing up and down but not from side to side

tropical year year length on which the **Gregorian Calendar** is based, equal in time to 365.242 days and shorter than a **sidereal year** because it takes into account the precession of the earth's **axis.**

tropics regions of the earth close to the **equator,** bounded by the lines of **latitude** 23.5° North and 23.5° South

Universal Time (UT) another name for **Greenwich Mean Time**

More Books to Read

Ganeri, Anita. *The Story of Time and Clocks.* New York: Oxford University Press, 1997.

Ganeri, Anita. *The Story of Maps and Navigation.* New York: Oxford University Press, 1998.

Pollard, Michael. *The Clock and How It Changed the World.* New York: Facts on File, 1995.

Index